BIRDLIKE
DINOSAURS!

Small Theropods and Prehistoric Birds

WORLD
BOOK

A Scott Fetzer company
Chicago
www.worldbook.com

For information about other World Book publications, visit our website at http://www.worldbookonline.com or call **1-800-WORLDBK (967-5325).**

For information about sales to schools and libraries, call **1-800-975-3250** (United States), or **1-800-837-5365** (Canada).

© 2013, 2006 Amber Books Ltd., London

World Book, Inc.
233 N. Michigan Ave.
Chicago, IL 60601

Amber Books Ltd.
74-77 White Lion Street
London N1 9PF
United Kingdom
www.amberbooks.co.uk

Library of Congress Cataloging-in-Publication Data
Birdlike dinosaurs : small Theropods and prehistoric birds.
  p. cm. -- (Dinosaurs!)
  Summary: "An introduction to small theropods, a group of dinosaurs that walked on two legs and that included the meat-eating dinosaurs, and to prehistoric birds. Features include an original drawing of each dinosaur, fun facts, a glossary, and a list of additional resources" -- Provided by publisher.
  Includes index.
  ISBN 978-0-7166-0368-9
  1. Saurischia--Juvenile literature. 2. Carnivorous animals, Fossil--Juvenile literature. 3. Birds--Evolution--Juvenile literature. 4. Paleontology--Jurassic--Juvenile literature. 5. Paleontology--Cretaceous--Juvenile literature. I. World Book, Inc.
  QE862.S3B575 2013
  567.912--dc23
                    2012016107
Dinosaurs!
Set ISBN 978-0-7166-0366-5
Printed in China by Toppan Leefung Printing Ltd., Guangdong Province
2nd printing October 2013

STAFF

Executive Committee

President
Donald D. Keller
Vice President and Editor in Chief
Paul A. Kobasa
Vice President of Sales & Marketing
Sean Lockwood
Vice President, International
Richard Flower
Director, Human Resources
Bev Ecker

Editorial

Associate Director,
  Supplementary Publications
Scott Thomas
Managing Editor,
  Supplementary Publications
Barbara A. Mayes
Editors
Michael Barr
Brian Johnson
Nicholas Kilzer
Kristina Vaicikonis
Researcher
Annie Brodsky
Administrative Assistant
Ethel Matthews
Manager, Indexing Services
David Pofelski
Manager, Contracts & Compliance
  (Rights & Permissions)
Loranne K. Shields

Editorial Administration

Director, Systems and Projects
Tony Tills
Senior Manager,
  Publishing Operations
Timothy Falk
Associate Manager,
  Publishing Operations
Audrey Casey

Manufacturing/Production

Director
Carma Fazio
Manufacturing Manager
Steven K. Hueppchen
Production/Technology Manager
Anne Fritzinger
Production Specialist
Curley Hunter
Proofreader
Emilie Schrage

Graphics and Design

Senior Manager
Tom Evans
Senior Designer
Don Di Sante

Product development
Amber Books Ltd.
Authors
Per Christiansen and Chris McNab
Designer
Jerry Williams

Contents

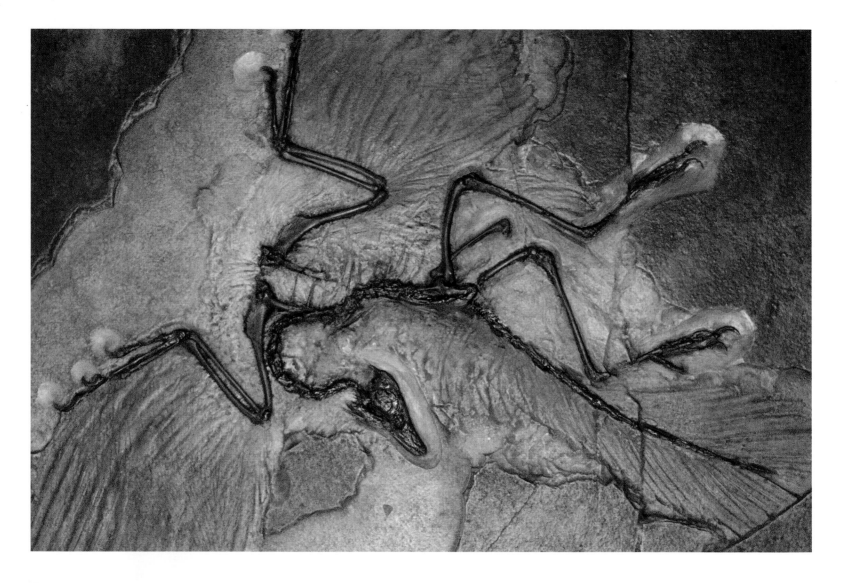

4

An egg *(above)* laid by the dinosaur Oviraptor was recovered from a nest, which the dinosaur guarded, much like a modern bird. A fossil of Archaeopteryx *(opposite)* preserves traces of feathers around the animal's body.

Introduction

An animal with black feathers watches from the trees, its eyes glittering in the gloom. It is hidden among the leaves of a great forest in what is now eastern Asia, about 120 million years ago. At first glance, the animal appears to be a bird. But as it climbs among the trees, it grips the bark with claws on both its hands and feet. Its jaws are lined with sharp teeth. It seems to have four wings, all with long feathers. When it stretches out its limbs to glide between the trees, it is plain that this animal is like no bird alive today. In fact, it is not a bird at all. It is Microraptor *(MY-kroh-RAP-tuhr)*, a magnificent feathered dinosaur. The discovery of Microraptor and other feathered dinosaurs has transformed our understanding of both dinosaurs and birds.

For many years, scientists thought that only birds had feathers—until a feathered dinosaur fossil was discovered in 1996. Other fossil discoveries soon revealed that a variety of small theropod *(THAIR-uh-pod)* dinosaurs had feathers. Most scientists now believe that feathers first appeared among these dinosaurs. In fact, birds descended from one group of feathered dinosaurs. In this sense, birds are feathered dinosaurs themselves.

Theropods were a diverse group of dinosaurs that typically walked upright on their two hind legs. Their relatively short arms ended in hands that could grasp objects. Most had a long, muscular tail to provide balance. However, theropods varied greatly in size. The largest theropods were far longer and heavier than any *predator* (meat-eater) alive today, reaching more than 40 feet

(12 meters) long. But other theropods were smaller. Many of the theropods included in this book resembled an ostrich, in both size and body shape. The smallest theropods were only about the size of a crow.

Birdlike dinosaurs appeared some time in the Jurassic Period, near the middle of the Age of Dinosaurs, which lasted from about 251 million to 65 million years go. Earth went through great changes during this time. In the beginning, a vast supercontinent that scientists call Pangaea *(pan-JEE-uh)* was surrounded by a great ocean. Pangaea broke apart over millions of years, and the continents drifted toward the positions they occupy today. There also were great changes among plants and animals. Such seed plants as conifers, cycads, and ginkgoes were common early in the Age of Dinosaurs. The first true mammals appeared, and crocodilians, frogs, insects, and lizards grew

The Age of Dinosaurs

Period	Triassic	Jurassic	Cretaceous
Began	251 million years ago	200 million years ago	145 million years ago
Ended	200 million years ago	145 million years ago	65 million years ago
Major Events	Dinosaurs first appeared but did not become common until the end of this period.	Dinosaurs became the largest animals everywhere on land reaching their greatest size.	A mass extinction at the end of this period killed off all the dinosaurs except some birds.

Dinosaurs appeared during the Triassic Period. They became the largest, most successful land animals early in the Jurassic Period. Dinosaurs died out at the end of the Cretaceous Period. Together, these three periods make up the Mesozoic Era, the Age of Dinosaurs.

200 million years ago

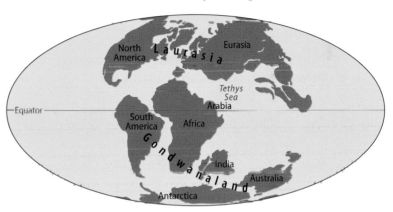

Eurasia

Panthalassa
Ocean

North
America

Pangaea

Tethys
Sea

Arabia

South
America

Africa

India

Panthalassa
Ocean

Equator

Antarctica

Australia

100 million years ago

North
America

Laurasia

Eurasia

Tethys
Sea

Arabia

South
America

Africa

Gondwanaland

India

Equator

Australia

Antarctica

About 200 million years ago (above left) a supercontinent that scientists call Pangaea was surrounded by a vast ocean. Pangaea broke up into separate continents during the Age of Dinosaurs. By 100 million years ago (above right), the continents had begun to drift toward the positions they occupy today.

numerous. Flying reptiles called pterosaurs (TEHR-uh-sawrz) filled the skies. Plesiosaurs (PLEE-see-uh-sawrz) and other marine reptiles prowled the oceans. Later, flowering plants appeared and began to replace other seed plants in some areas, helping insects and mammals to thrive.

Birdlike dinosaurs thrived up until the end of the Cretaceous Period, about 65 million years ago. At that time, many animals and plants became extinct, including all the dinosaurs except for certain birds. The surviving birds soon developed into many different types and spread around the world. Today, birds are the last living trace of the mighty dinosaurs that once ruled Earth.

Sinosauropteryx was a birdlike dinosaur covered in simple, downy feathers, with reddish and white stripes down its tail *(left)*. Shadows along the back and tail of a Sinosauropteryx fossil are traces of feathers *(opposite)*.

8

Small Theropods

Early birdlike dinosaurs were predators that grew to about the size of a turkey. These small theropods gave rise to a variety of other birdlike dinosaurs of different sizes and with different ways of life.

Many birdlike dinosaurs resembled fierce ostriches. They were light, graceful animals that could run quickly to escape predators. Other birdlike dinosaurs, like Velociraptor, were fearsome predators. Velociraptor had long, intimidating claws on its hind feet that it could use to slash at prey.

These small theropods were like birds in several ways. Their skeletons were similar to those of birds. Most of them probably dug nests in the ground and guarded their eggs. Many birdlike dinosaurs had relatively large brains and were likely intelligent. Like birds, they may have been warm-blooded, which would have made them active and quick.

Many birdlike dinosaurs also may have had feathers. Feathers and other soft tissues are usually not preserved in fossils, but in rare cases, scientists have discovered traces of feathers around dinosaur skeletons. Many of these feathers are simple, like a downy fuzz. Others are more complex, resembling modern flight feathers. Some feathers are so well preserved that scientists can even reconstruct their color. However, in most cases, scientists cannot say for certain whether a particular kind of dinosaur had feathers.

Compsognathus

(KOMP-sog-NAY-thus)

Compsognathus grew to about the size of a turkey. It had a light body with birdlike feet and short arms. Compsognathus was almost certainly covered in feathers.

Ornitholestes

(or-NITH-oh-LES-teez)

Ornitholestes was a light, slender theropod, which grew somewhat larger than Compsognathus. It had relatively long arms that it could use to grab swift prey.

FUN FACT

Coelurus was among the first birdlike dinosaurs discovered by scientists. Birdlike dinosaurs are also called coelurosaurs in its honor.

Coelurus

(see-LURE-us)

Coelurus was a swift theropod that lived about 150 million years ago. Scientists first discovered fossils of Coelurus in Wyoming in the 1870's.

Sinosauropteryx

(SYN-oh-sawr-AHP-tuh-rihks) was the first dinosaur known to have feathers. These simple, downy feathers provided insulation and may have been important for courtship or other displays. Sinosauropteryx was only about the size of a chicken, growing up to 3 feet (0.9 meter) long.

Alternating bands of reddish and white stripes covered the tail.

Sinosauropteryx had a very long, bony tail that provided balance when the dinosaur was running.

FACT○SAUR

Scientists have determined Sinosauropteryx's coloration by studying fossils of its feathers with a powerful microscope.

www.worldbook.com/dino16

Pelicanimimus

(PEL-uh-kan-uh-MIME-us)
Pelicanimimus had a deep pouch beneath its lower jaw, like a modern-day pelican. It may have waded into lakes to catch fish. Its jaws held more than 200 tiny teeth, the most of any known theropod.

Harpymimus

(HAR-pee-MIME-us)
Harpymimus was an early ostrichlike dinosaur. It had a small skull and long neck. Unlike later ostrichlike dinosaurs, its bill held some teeth.

Utahraptor

(YOO-tah-RAP-tor)
Utahraptor was an unusually large birdlike dinosaur, growing up to 23 feet (7 meters) long. It could slash open prey with the long, sharp claws on its hind feet.

Garudimimus

(ga-ROOD-uh-MIME-us)
Garudimimus had a toothless bill and likely ate both plants and animals. It had relatively heavy feet and weak legs, so it was not as swift as many later birdlike dinosaurs.

Alvarezsaurus

(al-vuh-rez-SAWR-us)
Alvarezsaurus had birdlike legs and a very long tail. It could run quickly to escape predators. It likely fed on insects.

Deinonychus

(die-NON-ih-kus)
Deinonychus could slash open prey with its claws. A single long claw grew on each hind foot. This relative of Velociraptor may have been covered in feathers.

FUN FACT

Deinonychus and its relatives walked with their long claws held above the ground, to keep them sharp.

Erlikosaurus

(ER-lik-oh-SAWR-us)
Erlikosaurus was a plant-eating theropod with long, thin claws. It was a close relative of Nanshiungosaurus.

Nanshiungosaurus

(NAN-shee-ung-ah-SAWR-us)
Nanshiungosaurus belongs to an unusual group of theropods that fed mainly on plants. These dinosaurs had long claws that were likely used for defense and to tear plants.

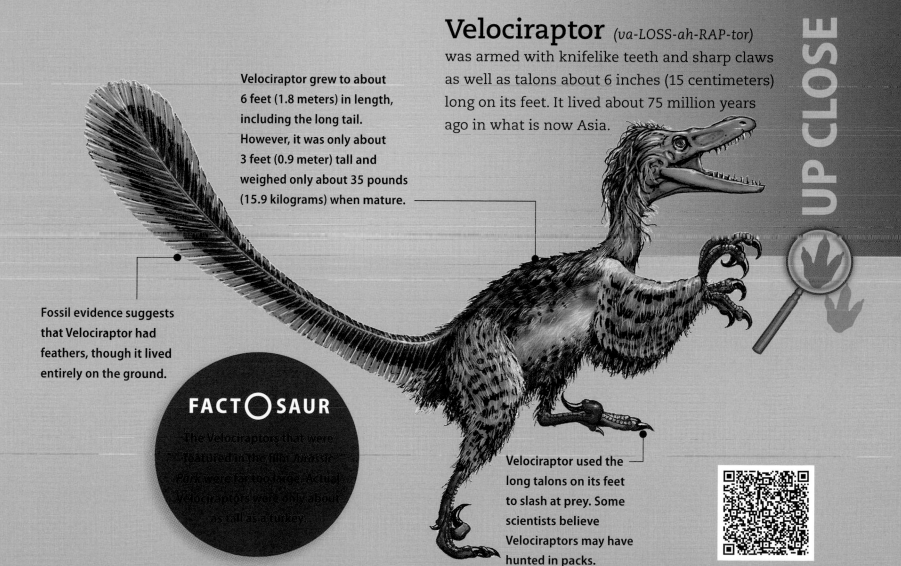

Velociraptor (va-LOSS-ah-RAP-tor)

was armed with knifelike teeth and sharp claws as well as talons about 6 inches (15 centimeters) long on its feet. It lived about 75 million years ago in what is now Asia.

Velociraptor grew to about 6 feet (1.8 meters) in length, including the long tail. However, it was only about 3 feet (0.9 meter) tall and weighed only about 35 pounds (15.9 kilograms) when mature.

Fossil evidence suggests that Velociraptor had feathers, though it lived entirely on the ground.

FACT○SAUR

The Velociraptors that were featured in the film *Jurassic Park* were far too large. Actual Velociraptors were only about as tall as a turkey.

Velociraptor used the long talons on its feet to slash at prey. Some scientists believe Velociraptors may have hunted in packs.

www.worldbook.com/dino17

Conchoraptor

(KONK-oh-RAP-tor)
The roof of this dinosaur's mouth was covered with bony bumps. It may have used the bumps to break open shellfish and tough dinosaur eggs.

Therizinosaurus

(THER-uh-ZEEN-oh-SAWR-us)
Therizinosaurus had arms more than 10 feet (3 meters) long. Its claws, which reached more than 3 feet (0.9 meter) in length, were far longer than those of any animal alive today. Despite these fearsome claws, this relative of Nanshiungosaurus ate mainly plants.

Oviraptor *(OH-vi-RAP-tor)* was a swift, birdlike dinosaur that lived in what is now Asia. It grew to about 7 feet (2.1 meters) long but weighed only 90 pounds (40 kilograms). Its name means "egg robber," because scientists mistakenly thought it lived on eggs it stole from other dinosaurs.

Oviraptor had a bony crest on its head. This crest was too weak to serve as armor. Scientists believe it was likely used for display, possibly to attract mates.

Oviraptor had a strong, toothless bill that may have been used to crack open nuts or shellfish.

FACT◯SAUR

Scientists thought Oviraptor stole eggs because they found it in a nest, but they later learned Oviraptor, like modern birds, was acutally guarding its own eggs.

17

Gallimimus (*gal-uh-MIME-us*) resembled an oversized ostrich, growing to about 20 feet (6 meters) long and weighing up to 440 pounds (200 kilograms). Gallimimus lived 70 million years ago in what is now Asia.

Like an ostrich, Gallimimus had powerful legs that enabled it to run quickly and escape predators.

Gallimimus had no teeth in its bill. Some scientists believe it filtered lake and pond water for tiny animals, as many ducks do today. Others think it probably fed on plant matter.

FACTOSAUR

The name Gallimimus means "rooster mimic," which refers to the dinosaur's birdlike skeleton. But it was much larger than a rooster.

18

Borogovia

(bor-oh-GOH-vee-a)
Borogovia was a small predator that likely ambushed prey, slashing with the claws on its three-fingered hands.

Chirostenotes

(KIE-roh-STEN-oh-teez)
Chirostenotes was a swift relative of Oviraptor that lived in what is now North America. It probably chased down small mammals and reptiles.

Adasaurus

(ADD-ah-SAWR-us)
Like its close relative Velociraptor, Adasaurus used the claws on its hind feet to attack prey. Adasaurus was about the size of a large dog.

Archaeornithomimus

(*AHR-kee-or-NITH-oh-MIME-us*)
Fossilized footprints in China sugget that this dinosaur could run at speeds of up to 43 miles (69 kilometers) per hour, about as fast as a race horse.

Anserimimus

(*AN-ser-i-MIME-us*)
Anserimimus was an ostrich-like dinosaur with unusually long forelimbs. It grew to only about 3 feet (0.9 meter) long and probably ate dinosaur eggs or small animals.

FACT◯SAUR

Chinese Palentologist Xu Xing found Gigantoraptor in 2005, as he reenacted the discovery of another dinosaur fossil for a Japanese film crew.

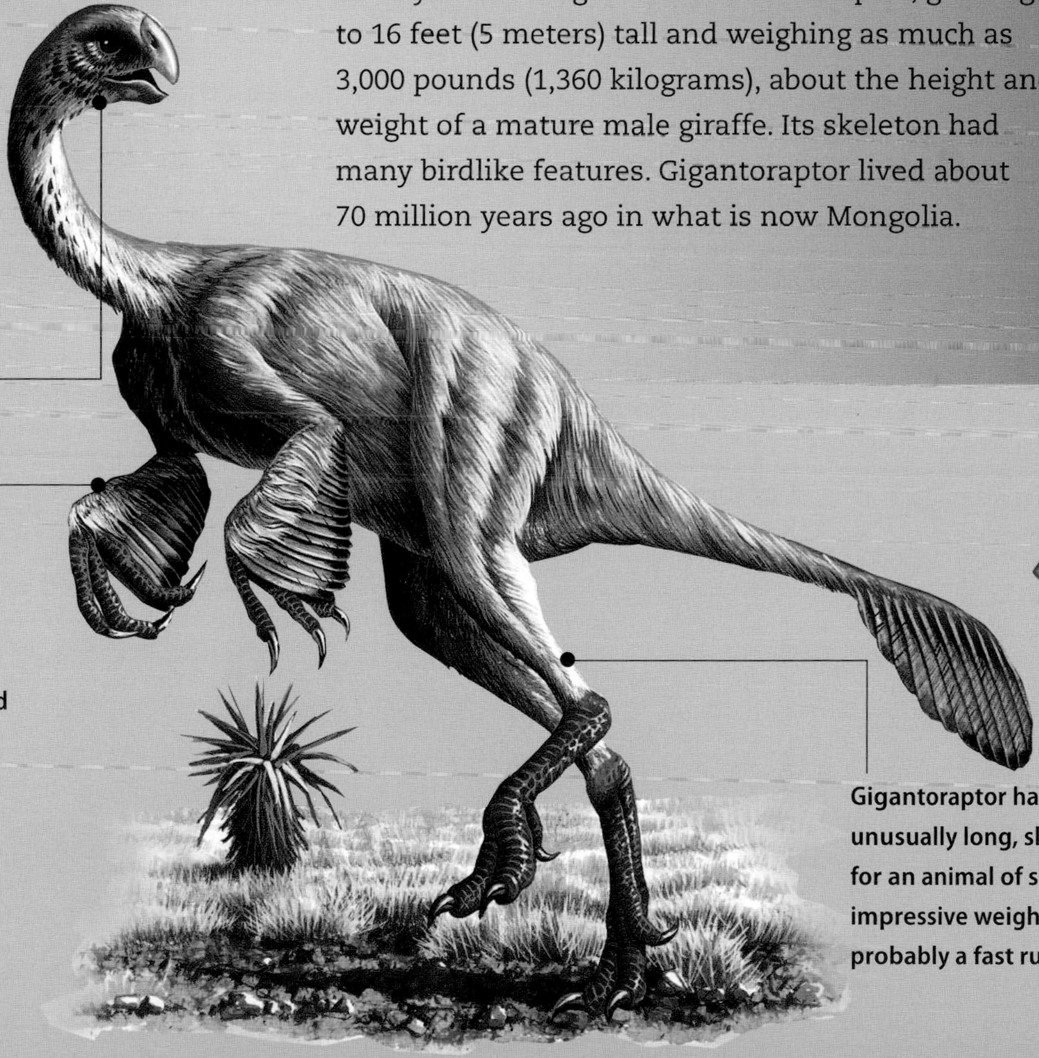

Gigantoraptor (jy-GAN-toh-RAP-tuhr)

was by far the largest relative of Oviraptor, growing up to 16 feet (5 meters) tall and weighing as much as 3,000 pounds (1,360 kilograms), about the height and weight of a mature male giraffe. Its skeleton had many birdlike features. Gigantoraptor lived about 70 million years ago in what is now Mongolia.

Gigantoraptor had a strong, toothless bill. Scientists are not sure whether it ate plants or chased down prey.

Gigantoraptor may have had feathers on its wings and possibly its tail. These feathers were likely used mainly for display.

Gigantoraptor had unusually long, slender legs for an animal of such impressive weight. It was probably a fast runner.

21

Saurornithoides

(*SAWR-or-NITH-oy-dees*)
Saurornithoides was a close relative of Troodon and was similar in most respects, though it lived in what is now Asia rather than what is now North America.

Struthiomimus

(*STROOTH-ee-o-MIME-us*)
Struthiomimus ran quickly on its long legs, holding its tail out for balance. It probably relied on speed to escape tyrannosaurs and other predators.

FUN FACT

Struthiomimus lived in what is now Canada and had to tolerate cool winters, though at that time, temperatures did not fall as low as they do today.

A long, whiplike tail provided balance when Troodon was running.

Troodon *(TROH-oh-don)* was a birdlike theropod that lived in what is now North America about 70 million years ago. Troodon had a large brain and was probably one of the most intelligent dinosaurs. The name Troodon means "wounding tooth," a reference to the dinosaur's 120 saw-edged teeth, which could cut through the toughest skin.

Troodon had large eyes that faced forward, suggesting it relied on keen eyesight to hunt. It could likely see well in low light and may have even hunted at night.

Strong hind legs allowed Troodon to chase down small prey. These dinosaurs may have hunted in packs.

FACT○SAUR

Troodon laid up to two dozen eggs in a nest dug in the ground. Parents guarded the eggs and kept them warm, much as birds do today.

23

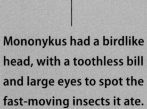

Mononykus (mo-NON-i-kus) was a

birdlike theropod. It was tiny, less than 3 feet (0.9 meter) long, and weighed less than 6 pounds (2.7 kilograms). Unlike most other theropods, Mononykus had only one digit on its hands. It lived in what is now Mongolia about 67 million years ago.

Mononykus was likely covered in simple feathers, which may have helped it to stay warm. Scientists do not actually know the color of its feathers. ⌐

FACT◯SAUR

Mononykus had the shortest arms of any known dinosaur. Unlike other theropods, it had only one visible claw on each hand.

The arms were short but powerful. Each ended in a single banana-shaped claw. Mononykus may have used its claws for ripping into termite nests. It might then have slurped up the insects with its tongue.

Mononykus had a birdlike head, with a toothless bill and large eyes to spot the fast-moving insects it ate.

Dromiceiomimus

(DROH-mee-see-uh-MIME-us)
Dromiceiomimus was a close relative of Struthiomimus. Its light body and long, powerful legs enabled it to run quicky.

Noasaurus

(NOH-ah-SAWR-us)
Noasaurus was a swift predator that may have hunted in packs. The long claws found with a fossilized skeleton may have grown on the hands rather than the feet.

Elmisaurus

(ELM-ee-SAWR-us)
Elmisaurus was another slender, ostrichlike theropod that relied on speed and its sharp claws to catch prey.

DINO BITE

The Origin of Feathers

Feathers rank among nature's great innovations. Feathers keep such songbirds as cardinals warm even in deep winter, when temperatures plunge far below freezing. Feathers almost never break in flight, even among falcons that dive at speeds of more than 200 miles (320 kilometers) per hour. Feathers can also be beautiful, such as the brilliant feathers the peacock uses to attract mates.

For many years, scientists thought feathers were unique to birds, but a series of remarkable discoveries has shown that feathers first appeared among dinosaurs.

Feathers are rarely preserved in fossils. It was only in 1996 that *paleontologists* (scientists who study prehistoric life) found proof that a dinosaur had feathers. A 125-million-year-old fossil preserved the skeleton of a small theropod dinosaur named Sinosauropteryx. The fossil also preserved traces of feathers. The claim that a dinosaur had feathers was controversial. Eventually, additional fossil discoveries convinced most paleontologists that many theropod dinosaurs had feathers.

Feathers may have originated among small theropods in the Jurassic Period. Some scientists believe feathers appeared even earlier. The earliest feathers were probably bundles of simple strands, like down. These short, fuzzy feathers were not useful for flight. Instead, feathers may have provided insulation, or they may have been important for courtship or other displays.

Some dinosaurs developed larger and more complex feathers. These feathers had a stiff central shaft lined with many strands. These feathers were

The Ruppell's vulture *(above)* relies on downy feathers to keep it warm. Its flight feathers enable the vulture to soar high above the ground for hours at a time.

not as sophisticated as modern flight feathers, but they would have enabled dinosaurs to glide between trees. Many scientists think birds descended from such a feathered dinosaur. Birds became better fliers over time, as both their feathers and bodies became adapted to flight.

Throughout the late Jurassic and the Cretaceous periods, birds and feathered dinosaurs lived side by side. Sinosauropteryx had only simple, downy feathers. Yet it lived long after Anchiornis, a birdlike theropod with crude flight feathers that lived about 160 million years ago. Because Anchiornis had more complex feathers, paleontologists believe feathers must have originated even earlier, among dinosaurs that remain unknown to science.

New research methods also have played a role in understanding feathers. In 2010, scientists reconstructed the color of some dinosaur feathers by examining them with a powerful microscope. The microscope revealed complex arrays of *melanosomes* (tiny pigment-bearing structures in cells). Melanosomes give modern bird feathers much of their coloration. By comparing the arrangement of melanosomes in dinosaur feathers with those of modern birds, scientists were able determine their color. Thus, we know that Anchiornis had mainly gray feathers, with black-and-white feathers on the limbs. Sinosauropteryx had mainly reddish and white feathers, with stripes down its back.

Paleontologists continue to search for fossils of feathered dinosaurs and prehistoric birds. Each new discovery brings us closer to understanding the origin of both feathers and birds.

The Rise of Birds

The first known feathered theropods appeared in the Jurassic Period. Some of these dinosaurs almost certainly lived in the trees. They likely used their feathers and winglike limbs to glide between trees, both to feed and to escape predators. Birds are thought to descend from one of these feathered, tree-dwelling dinosaurs.

The precise origin of birds remains unknown, but they probably appeared more than 160 million years ago. Scientists still debate the classification of the earliest feathered theropods. It is not always clear whether these animals were birds or very close relatives of birds. Some scientists even argue that Archaeopteryx, the most famous early bird, may actually have been a small, feathered dinosaur rather than a true bird.

Birds flourished throughout the Cretaceous Period. They became much more diverse, adapting to a variety of environments. There were large diving birds that fed on fish, eaglelike birds that hunted small animals, and small birds that ate only plants. Many birds of the Cretaceous Period were unlike any modern bird, having claws on their wings, a bony tail, and a bill filled with sharp teeth. Others probably looked much like the birds we see today.

Confuciousornis had claws on its wings *(right)*, like many other birds from the Age of Dinosaurs. Scientists have found thousands of fossils of Confuciousornis *(opposite)*.

Anchiornis

(AN-kee-AWR-nihs)
Anchiornis had crude flight feathers on both its long fore-limbs and hindlimbs. Scientists have reconstructed the color of these feathers through the study of *melanosomes* (tiny pigment-bearing structures in cells). Anchiornis lived about 160 million years ago.

Epidexipteryx

(EHP-ee-dehks-IHP-tuhr-ihks)
Epidexipteryx had four long feathers on its tail. These were mainly used for display, though they also may have provided balance in the trees. The long fingers may have helped it to catch insect grubs.

Xiaotingia

(show-TIHNG-jyah)
Xiaotingia was a very early bird or a closely related dinosaur. It resembled Archaeopteryx in most respects but appeared earlier, about 160 million years ago.

Archaeopteryx had sharp claws on its wings. Its strong flight feathers enabled it to glide between trees or possibly even fly. However, Archaeopteryx would not have been a strong flier.

Archaeopteryx (AHR-kee-OP-tuhr-ihks)

is the most famous bird from the Age of Dinosaurs, though some scientists think it was a closely related dinosaur rather than a true bird. This crow-sized animal likely spent much of its time in the trees. It lived in what is now Europe about 150 million years ago.

FACT○SAUR

Archaeopteryx was discovered in 1861. Its mix of bird and reptile traits provided support for Charles Darwin's new theory of evolution.

Archaeopteryx had the long, bony tail of a theropod, but the tail was covered in flight feathers.

The bill was lined with sharp teeth. Some scientists think Archaeopteryx may have fed on small pterosaurs.

www.worldbook.com/dino18

Microraptor (MY-kroh-RAP-tuhr)

was a feathered dinosaur that was closely related to birds. The long feathers on Microraptor's limbs would have enabled it to glide between trees or possibly even fly. It lived in what is now Asia about 120 million years ago.

Microraptor had black, shiny feathers, much like those of a crow. It had claws on its forelimbs.

Scientists continue to debate how Microraptor positioned its limbs in the air. Unlike any animal alive today, it had flight feathers on all four limbs.

Microraptor was even smaller than Archaeopteryx, growing to only about 2 feet (0.6 meter) long and about 1 foot (0.3 meter) tall.

FACT O SAUR

One Microraptor fossil appears to have a small bird in its stomach. Microraptor may have snatched birds from the trees or possibly even in midair.

www.worldbook.com/dino19

Sinornithosaurus

(SYN-*uhr-nihth-oh-SAWR-uhs*)

Sinornithosaurus was similar to Microraptor in size and way of life. Beautifully preserved fossils suggest it had striking reddish coloration. It lived in what is now Asia more than 120 million years ago.

Shanweiniao

(SAN-*way-NYOW*)

Shanweiniao was a bird that lived about 120 million years ago. It had fan-shaped tail feathers for improved flight, much like those of a modern bird. However, it belonged to a different group of birds, with no living descendants.

Confuciousornis

(*kuhn-FYOO-shuhs-AWR-nihs*)
Confuciousornis lacked teeth but had claws on its wings. Scientists have found thousands of its fossils, because it was one of the most common birds 125 million years ago.

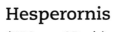

Hesperornis

(*HES-per-OR-nis*)
Hesperornis was a flightless diving bird that grew to about 6 feet (1.8 meters) long. It lived about 80 million years ago.

Like other prehistoric birds, Enantiornis had claws on its wings. But changes in its skeleton allowed it to fly with more agility, power, and efficiency than Confuciousornis and other earlier birds.

Enantiornis (ehn-an-tee-AWR-nihs)

resembled a turkey vulture in many respects, though it had teeth and claws on its wings. The wings reached about 4 feet (1.2 meters) across, making Enantiornis larger than most other birds from the Age of Dinosaurs. Enantiornis lived about 70 million years ago in what is now South America.

Enantiornis had sharp teeth in its bill. It may have been a scavenger that fed on animal remains. It may even have lived like a hawk, seizing small prey in its talons.

FACT○SAUR

Enantiornis belonged to the most diverse group of birds in the Cretaceous Period. All members of this group died out at the end of the Age of Dinosaurs.

www.worldbook.com/dino20

DINO BITE

Why Did Birds Survive?

Life on Earth suffered a catastrophe about 65 million years ago. Scientists have found strong evidence that an asteroid up to 6 miles (10 kilometers) wide struck in the area of present-day Mexico. The impact threw billions of tons of dust and debris into the atmosphere, darkening the skies for months and causing temperatures to plunge worldwide. Massive volcanic eruptions in present-day India added to the chaos. This turmoil caused many kinds of animals and plants to die out over a short period, an event called a mass extinction. Most famously, all the dinosaurs became extinct, except for certain types of birds. Scientists are not certain why those birds survived, while similar kinds of dinosaurs disappeared.

Birds had several traits that may have contributed to their survival. Nearly all of Earth's large animals died in the mass extinction, whether they were dinosaurs or other kinds of animals. Small animals, including birds, generally fared better. The feathers of birds could have kept them warm through the long, dark winter caused by the asteroid strike. In addition, many birds likely fed on seeds, decaying plant matter, or insects, which could have sustained them until conditions improved and plants began to recover. Birds also may have been able to fly away from areas of devastation, to warmer regions that still had food.

The mystery is that many other animals with similar advantages did not survive. Many small, feathered dinosaurs were like birds in most respects.

The cassowary *(above)* of New Guinea belongs to an ancient group of birds. Scientists do not know why certain birds survived the mass extinction that ended the Age of Dinosaurs.

They had feathers for warmth, and some could glide or possibly even fly. Many of these dinosaurs likely fed on foods similar to those eaten by birds. Scientists do not know why none of these dinosaurs survived.

In fact, most birds did not survive the great catastrophe. Many kinds of birds that flourished in the Cretaceous Period died out with the dinosaurs.

Scientists are not certain which groups of modern birds lived before the mass extinction. Some think several groups of modern birds had already appeared by the Late Cretaceous Period, including water fowl and certain flightless birds. Others think only a single group of birds survived the extinction. According to this view, the many kinds of birds alive today arose from this one group of survivors.

For the animals that did survive, the extinction created profound opportunities. Both birds and mammals quickly diversified and spread around the world. Mammals became the largest animals in most environments, taking on roles previously held by dinosaurs.

For the most part, birds thrived by being small. Perching birds are the most diverse group of modern birds, making up more than half of living bird species. Incredibly, many perching birds weigh less than 1 ounce (28 grams).

The dinosaurs ruled as giants, but their large size helped drive them to extinction. Most birds survive by being small and quick. The journey from mighty Tyrannosaurus to the delicate songbirds that thrive today is a triumph of adaptation, endurance, and good fortune.

DINO BITE

The Fossil Beds of Liaoning

Sinosauropteryx, a feathered dinosaur, stands on the shore of a shallow lake, cautiously sipping water. Plants unlike any known today grow on the rolling hills around the lake. In the distance, a plume of gray ash rises from a volcano. When a twig breaks in the surrounding forest, Sinosauropteryx flashes the bristly reddish feathers on its crest. Among the trees, a bird named Confuciusornis flaps its wings, exposing patches of black, orange-brown, and white coloring on its feathers. These are only two of the feathered animals that scientists have found in Liaoning (lee-ow-NING) Province in northeastern China. In fact, fossils from Liaoning have forever changed how scientists think about birds and dinosaurs.

In 1996, a Chinese farmer and amateur fossil hunter named Li Yumin discovered the first Sinosauropteryx fossil. Initially, scientists thought Sinosauropteryx was an early kind of bird. However, Sinosauropteryx lacked wings, and its feathers were simple strands. This animal was not a bird. Instead, it was a small theropod dinosaur. Scientists soon discovered many other feathered dinosaurs in the Liaoning fossil beds. These discoveries include such dinosaurs as Anchiornis and Microraptor. Most scientists now believe these fossils prove

that birds arose from dinosaurs. In fact, many theropods likely had feathers. Birds are simply a group of feathered dinosaurs that did not become extinct.

Liaoning is special because of the superb preservation of its fossils. Most dead animals never become fossils. When fossils do form, they usually preserve only some of the bones, which are often jumbled. Scientists must reconstruct the skeleton through painstaking effort. However, many fossils of Liaoning preserve entire skeletons, still arranged as if in life. Incredibly, some of these fossils even preserve feathers and other soft tissues.

Special conditions in Liaoning during the Age of Dinosaurs preserved these remarkable fossils. Over millions of years, volcanic eruptions covered the area in ash. Choked by volcanic gas, animals fell to the ground or into shallow water, where they were covered in ash and other volcanic material. This sediment protected these remains from decay, helping to create exquisite fossils.

Unfortunately, Liaoning's fame has carried a cost. The fossil boom has tempted some people to collect fossils illegally, to sell them. Such fossils are often collected improperly, which limits their scientific value. In addition, some people have tried to sell fake fossils as important Liaoning discoveries.

Still, scientists continue to discover magnificent fossils in Liaoning. In addition to feathered dinosaurs, the fossil beds preserve plants and a variety of other animals, including fish, insects, and mammals. In fact, fossils from Liaoning have enabled scientists to study whole communities of plants and animals, to understand how they lived with one another. Who knows what marvels remain hidden in the fossil beds of Liaoning?

Liaoning Province lies in northeastern China *(below)***. Paleontologist Xu Xing works to recover a fossil in one of the province's rich fossil beds** *(opposite)***.

Where to Find Dinosaurs

Museums in the United States

ARIZONA

Arizona Museum of Natural History
http://azmnh.org/Exhibits/dinohall
53 N. Macdonald
Mesa, Arizona 85201

Theropods, sauropods, and other dinosaurs rule at Dinosaur Hall. Visitors can also explore prehistoric Arizona in the Walk Through Time exhibit.

CALIFORNIA

Natural History Museum of Los Angeles County
http://www.nhm.org/site/explore-exhibits
900 Exposition Boulevard
Los Angeles, California 90007

After you explore the fossils and skeletons in Dinosaur Hall, get a behind-the-scenes look at how the exhibits are made in the Dino Lab.

University of California Museum of Paleontology
http://www.ucmp.berkeley.edu
1101 Valley Life Sciences Building
Berkeley, California 94720

Many of this museum's exhibits are viewable online as well as in person.

COLORADO

Denver Museum of Nature & Science
http://www.dmns.org
2001 Colorado Boulevard
Denver, Colorado 80205

Dynamic re-creations of ancient environments as well as hands-on fossils tell the story of prehistoric life.

Dinosaur National Monument
http://www.nps.gov/dino
4545 Hwy 40, Dinosaur National Monument
Dinosaur, Colorado 81610

Dinosaur National Monument is located in both Colorado and Utah. Its world-famous Carnegie Dinosaur Quarry, home to nearly 1,500 dinosaur fossils, is on the Utah side.

CONNECTICUT

Dinosaur State Park
http://www.dinosaurstatepark.org
400 West Street
Rocky Hill, Connecticut 06067

Here you will find one of the largest dinosaur track sites in North America. Visitors can also explore the Arboretum, which contains more than 250 species of plants—many dating back to prehistoric eras.

Yale Peabody Museum of Natural History
http://peabody.yale.edu
170 Whitney Avenue
New Haven, Connecticut 06511-8902

Don't miss the Great Hall of Dinosaurs with its famous "Age of Reptiles" mural—one of the largest in the world.

GEORGIA

Fernbank Museum of Natural History
http://www.fernbankmuseum.org
767 Clifton Road NE
Atlanta, Georgia 30307
See a Giganotosaurus and other dinosaurs in the Giants of the Mesozoic exhibit.

ILLINOIS

Chicago Children's Museum at Navy Pier
http://www.chicagochildrensmuseum.org
700 East Grand Avenue
Chicago, Illinois 60611
Kids of all ages can explore a re-creation of an actual dinosaur excavation, where you can search for bones in an excavation pit.

Discovery Center Museum
http://www.discoverycentermuseum.org
711 North Main Street
Rockford, Illinois 61103
Visitors will enjoy the simulated dinosaur dig at this children's museum.

The Field Museum
http://fieldmuseum.org
1400 S. Lake Shore Drive
Chicago, Illinois 60605
Chicago's Field Museum is home to Sue, the largest and most complete Tyrannosaurus rex skeleton ever discovered.

The Field Museum, Chicago, Illinois

INDIANA

The Dinosphere at the Children's Museum of Indianapolis
http://www.childrensmuseum.org/themuseum/dinosphere
3000 North Meridian Street
Indianapolis, Indiana 46208
Experience the world of the dinosaurs with family digs, fossil preparation, and sensory exhibits.

MAINE

Maine Discovery Museum
http://www.mainediscoverymuseum.org
74 Main Street
Bangor, Maine 04401
Young visitors to this children's museum can explore the world of paleontology at the museum's new Dino Dig exhibit.

MASSACHUSETTS

The Museum of Science, Boston
http://www.mos.org
1 Science Park
Boston, Massachusetts 02114
A 23-foot- (7-meter-) long Triceratops specimen, found in the Dakota Badlands, is just one of the fascinating fossils on display here.

MICHIGAN

University of Michigan Museum of Natural History
http://www.lsa.umich.edu/ummnh
1109 Geddes Avenue
Ann Arbor, Michigan 48109
Michigan's largest collection of prehistoric specimens can be found in the Museum of Natural History's rotunda and galleries.

Carnegie Museum of
Natural History,
Pittsburgh, Pennsylvania

MINNESOTA

The Science Museum of Minnesota

http://www.smm.org
120 W. Kellogg Boulevard
St. Paul, Minnesota 55102

Do some hands-on fossil exploration at the
Paleontology Lab, then get inside the jaws of a
giant T. rex to simulate its mighty bite!

MONTANA

The Museum of the Rockies

http://www.museumoftherockies.org
600 West Kagy Blvd
Bozeman, Montana 59717

This museum's Siebel Dinosaur Complex
houses one of the largest collections of dinosaur fossils in the world.

NEW MEXICO

The New Mexico Museum of Natural History
and Science

http://www.nmnaturalhistory.org
1801 Mountain Road NW
Albuquerque, New Mexico 87104

The Timetracks exhibit covers the Triassic,
Jurassic, and Cretaceous periods.

NEW YORK

The American Museum of Natural History

http://www.amnh.org
Central Park West at 79th Street
New York, New York 10024

This museum's famous Fossil and Dinosaur
halls house nearly 1 million specimens.

NORTH CAROLINA

North Carolina Museum of Natural Sciences

http://naturalsciences.org

11 West Jones Street
Raleigh, North Carolina 27601

Home to Willo the Thescalosaurus, an
Acrocanthosaurus, and four fossilized whales.

PENNSYLVANIA

The Academy of Natural Sciences of
Drexel University

http://www.ansp.org/visit/exhibits/
dinosaur-hall
1900 Benjamin Franklin Parkway
Philadelphia, Pennsylvania 19103

Impressive skeletons of massive dinosaurs
stalk Drexel's Dinosaur Hall. Visitors can also visit
the fossil lab to learn how fossils are
prepared and studied.

The Carnegie Museum of Natural History

http://www.carnegiemnh.org/exhibitions/
dinosaurs.html
4400 Forbes Avenue
Pittsburgh, Pennsylvania 15213

The Dinosaurs in the Their Time exhibit features
scientifically accurate re-creations of environments from the Age of Dinosaurs..

SOUTH DAKOTA

The Children's Museum of South Dakota

http://www.prairieplay.org
521 4th Street
Brookings, South Dakota 57006

Meet Mama and Max, a pair of full-sized
animatronic T. rex dinosaurs, and try your
hand at a dinosaur dig.

TENNESSEE

Creative Discovery Museum
http://www.cdmfun.org
321 Chestnut Street
Chattanooga, Tennessee 37402

The Creative Discovery Museum's Excavation Station lets young visitors dig their own dinosaur bones.

TEXAS

The Houston Museum of Natural Science
http://www.hmns.org
5555 Hermann Park Drive
Houston, Texas 77030

The world-class Hall of Paleontology includes more than 30 dinosaurs and many other prehistoric creatures in "action" poses.

UTAH

The Natural History Museum of Utah
http://nhmu.utah.edu
301 Wakara Way
Salt Lake City, Utah 84108

The paleontology collections at Utah's Natural History Museum include more than 30,000 specimens.

VIRGINIA

The Virginia Museum of Natural History
http://www.vmnh.net
21 Starling Avenue
Martinsville, Virginia 24112

Detailed models and interactive features accompany the dinosaur exhibits.

WASHINGTON, D.C.

The National Museum of Natural History—Smithsonian Institution
http://www.mnh.si.edu
10th Street & Constitution Avenue NW
Washington, D.C. 20560

Visit the Hall of Paleontology—free of charge—to come face-to-face with dinosaurs, fossil mammals, and fossil plants.

WYOMING

The Wyoming Dinosaur Center
http://www.wyodino.org
110 Carter Ranch Road
Thermopolis, Wyoming 82443

The combined museum and dig site offers daylong digs for visitors of all ages.

The National Museum of Natural History, Smithsonian Institution, Washington, D.C.

Museums in Canada

ALBERTA

The Royal Tyrrell Museum
http://www.tyrrellmuseum.com
1500 North Dinosaur Trail
Drumheller, Alberta T0J 0Y0, Canada

Tyrannosaurus rex, Triceratops, Quetzalcoatlus (a pterodactyloid), and many other fossils can be found here.

ONTARIO

The Canadian Museum of Nature
http://nature.ca/en/home
240 McLeod Street
Ottawa, Ontario, Canada

Explore the lives—and the eventual extinction—of the dinosaurs in the Fossil Gallery.

The London Children's Museum
http://www.londonchildrensmuseum.ca
21 Wharncliffe Road South
London, Ontario N6J 4G5, Canada

The Dinosaur Gallery includes demonstrations, fossil casts, and replicas of many dinosaurs from the Jurassic Period.

The Royal Ontario Museum
http://www.rom.on.ca
100 Queen's Park
Toronto, Ontario, M5S 2C6, Canada

These exhibits feature dinosaurs and other fossils from the Jurassic and Cretaceous periods.

QUEBEC

The Redpath Museum
http://www.mcgill.ca/redpath
859 Sherbrooke Street West
Montreal, Quebec, Canada

Learn about the animals that roamed prehistoric Quebec as well as about many types of dinosaur.

Museums in the United Kingdom

Dinosaurland Fossil Museum
http://www.dinosaurland.co.uk/
Coombe Street, Lyme Regis
Dorset, DT7 3PY, United Kingdom

Dinosaurland includes a large collection of Jurassic fossils and dinosaur models.

The Dinosaur Museum
http://www.thedinosaurmuseum.com/
Icen Way, Dorchester
Dorset, DT1 1EW, United Kingdom

Highlights include kid-friendly, hands-on computer displays, dinosaur skeletons, and a wide range of fossils.

The National Museum of Scotland
http://www.nms.ac.uk/
Chambers Street
Edinburgh, EH1 1JF, United Kingdom

Allosaurus and Triceratops skeletons are part of a prehistory exhibit, along with dinosaur footprints and a "dino dig" for young visitors.

The Natural History Museum
http://www.nhm.ac.uk/
Cromwell Road, London SW7 5BD

The elaborate dinosaur gallery includes four animatronic dinosaurs.

Oxford University Museum of Natural History
http://www.oum.ox.ac.uk/
Parks Road, Oxford,
OX1 3PW, United Kingdom

The outstanding collection of dinosaur fossils and skeletons includes a Camptosaurus, Cetiosaurus, Eustreptospondylus, Iguanodon, Lexovisaurus, Megalosaurus, and a Metriacanthosaurus.

Museums in Australia

The Australian Museum
http://australianmuseum.net.au
6 College Street, Sydney
New South Wales 2010, Australia

A permanent dinosaur exhibit features high-tech interactive displays, animatronic dinosaurs, and a paleontology lab that is open to young visitors.

The Melbourne Museum
http://museumvictoria.com.au/
melbournemuseum
11 Nicholson St. Carlton
Victoria, 3053, Australia

A kid-friendly Dinosaur Walk exhibition brings the prehistoric world to life.

National Dinosaur Museum
http://www.nationaldinosaurmuseum.com.au
Gold Creek Road and Barton Highway
Nicholls, Australia Capital Terrority 2913,
Australia

Home to the largest permanent display of dinosaur and other prehistoric fossil material in Australia.

The South Australian Museum
http://www.samuseum.sa.gov.au
North Terrace
Adelaide, South Australia 5000, Australia

Walk through a paleontology collection that includes more than 40,000 specimens.

Royal Tyrrell Museum,
Drumheller, Canada
(opposite)

The Australian Museum,
Sydney, Australia *(left)*

Museums in New Zealand

The Canterbury Museum
http://www.canterburymuseum.com/
Christchurch Central, Christchurch 8013,
New Zealand

The Geology gallery features fossils and an introduction to the fearsome marine reptiles of New Zealand's prehistory.

Additional Resources

Books

Dinosaur Discovery: Everything You Need to Be a Paleontologist
by Christopher McGowan and Erica Lyn Schmidt (Simon and Schuster Books for Young Readers, 2011)

Activities and experiments show readers how paleontologists examine ancient fossils.

Dinosaur Mountain: Digging into the Jurassic Age
by Deborah Kogan Ray (Frances Foster Books/Farrar, Straus, Giroux, 2010)

Follow fossil expert Earl Douglass on his 1908 hunt for dinosaur bones, which led to the discovery of several amazing skeletons.

Dinosaurs
by John A. Long (Simon and Schuster Books for Young Readers, 2007)

3-D model imaging helps bring dinosaurs to life in this informative book.

Dinosaurs: The Most Complete, Up-to-Date Encyclopedia for Dinosaur Lovers of All Ages
by Thomas R. Holtz and Luis V. Rey (Random House, 2007)

A reference guide to all things dinosaur, from fossil hunting to evolution.

The Discovery and Mystery of a Dinosaur Named Jane
by Judith Williams (Enslow Publishers, 2008)

This book traces the journey of one dinosaur's skeleton, from discovery to museum.

DVD's

Bizarre Dinosaurs
(National Geographic, 2009)

Paleontologists lead you on a tour of some of the strangest dinosaurs to ever walk the Earth.

Dinosaur Collection
(Discovery-Gaiam, 2011)

Computer-animated simulations paint a vivid picture of dinosaurs and their world.

Dinosaurs Unearthed
(National Geographic, 2007)

Watch the examination of a mummified dinosaur for a new understanding of how dinosaurs looked, moved, and lived.

Index

Photo Credits